Classical Guitar Music of Antonio Vivaldi

arranged by Joseph Harris

TABLE OF CONTENTS

Catalog #07- 4090
ISBN# 1-56922-194-4

Printed in the United States of America   **Produced by John L. Haag**

HAL•LEONARD CORPORATION
7777 W. BLUEMOUND RD. P.O. BOX 13819 MILWAUKEE, WI 53213

Historical Notes & Performance Suggestions

For many years remembered only for his contribution of hundreds of violin concertos, Antonio Vivaldi is regarded today as a key musical figure of the Italian Baroque. Although his most visible and enduring influence was indeed in the development of the solo concerto, Vivaldi was also admired in his day as a composer of excellent chamber music, a stunning violinist and a popular composer of Italian opera. This composer of "The Four Seasons" was a bold and impetuous individual who managed to focus his musical impulses in a unique voice that was consistent yet expressive.

Vivaldi was born in Venice in 1678 and trained for the priesthood, but ended up practicing this vocation for only a brief time. Vivaldi served for nearly forty years (from 1703 until just before his death in 1741) as musical director of the *Conservatorio dell'Ospedale della Pietà,* one of four girls' orphanages in Venice. The *Ospedale* provided outstanding musical instruction and under Vivaldi's direction created quite a musical sensation. Vivaldi's tasks at the *Ospedale* included teaching private lessons, composing music for both concerts and church services, repairing musical instruments and commissioning works from other composers for concerts at the *Ospedale.*

Vivaldi was extremely prolific, composing over 50 operas, 90 sonatas and 450 concertos. Despite the apparent ease with which he could produce a composition (he once boasted he could compose a piece faster than it could be copied), Vivaldi is criticized sometimes for being too predictable. The twentieth-century Italian composer Luigi Dallapiccola once asserted that Vivaldi did not compose 450 separate concertos, but wrote the same concerto 450 times. Whereas during the Baroque many musicians believed that the particular intent of a composition (church, chamber or theatre) should dictate its musical language, Vivaldi's style varied little between genres and even between mediums. His vocal music and instrumental music share similar musical characteristics, as do his sacred and secular works. Furthermore, Vivaldi's compositional style remained remarkably consistent throughout his career and evolved very little. The only major variances one finds are in surface details, such as melodic contour, which tended to reflect public tastes. However, it is a tribute to Vivaldi's skill as a composer that within such a limited musical vocabulary he exhibited a virtually inexhaustible variety of invention.

Sonatas for Violin, Op. 2

The 12 Sonatas for Violin, Op. 2 were Vivaldi's first solo sonatas. The Sonatas were published in Italy in 1709 and dedicated to Frederick IV of Denmark on the occasion of his visit to Venice. For the Sonatas, Vivaldi drew upon models of Arcangelo Corelli, a conservative Italian composer whose works are tidily constructed, yet highly expressive. Vivaldi's Sonatas are a composite of church and chamber styles, demonstrating his tendency to blur boundaries between genres. In the Sonatas, dance movements intermingle with abstract movements (those with only tempo designations).

Baroque dances of the Italian variety differ considerably from their French or German equivalents. The slight differences in the names of dances (for example, compare the Italian *giga* to the French *gigue*) do not signify nationality only, but salient musical traits. Whereas the French *gigue* is a lively, bouncy dance in an imitative texture, the Italian *giga* has a more restrained sense of pulse, a less rhythmically active bass line and little or no imitation between voices. The Italian *gavotta* lacks the characteristic two upbeats and *musette*-like middle section of the French *gavotte*. The Italian *corrente* is faster and more "running" in character than the French *courante*. Also, the French *courante* may emphasize dotted rhythms and an alternation between duple and triple meter, while the *corrente* is more rhythmically consistent and metrically stable.

Sonata No. 3
In the *Adagio* (found on page 7), the bass line should be played with a warm tone, especially in areas where it is exposed (as in the opening and in measure 9). To achieve a warm tone on the guitar, play with the right hand close to the fretboard and strike the string with the side of the thumb, using as much flesh as possible. The *Giga* (found on page 8) should be played dynamically strong throughout and in a lightning fast tempo.

Sonata No. 6

The *Preludio* (found on page 12) should sound very elegant and graceful. Exaggerate the dotted rhythms by playing the long notes longer and the short notes shorter. The *Giga* (found on page 16) should be played in a moderately fast tempo. Count two beats per measure, not four, to give the piece a stronger and more stable sense of forward motion

Sonata No. 7

The tempo of the *Corrente* (found on page 19) should be very fast. However, in areas where the bass line becomes more active (especially in mm. 17-21), make sure that neither voice breaks down.

Sonata No. 9

The *Preludio* (found on page 23) is an energetic and dramatic piece. The movement contains elements of a "learned" style, which show off a composer's contrapuntal skills. Be sure to emphasize the points of imitation (as in the first few measures).

Sonata No. 11

The abundance of syncopated rhythms presents an interesting technical problem for the solo performer in the *Gavotta* (found on page 28). In order to convey the meter clearly, keep the tempo steady and count two beats per measure. Hold on to notes with the left hand for as long as possible before fingering new notes.

Sonatas for One or Two Violins, Op. 5

The Six Sonatas, Op. 5 were first published in 1716. By this time, Vivaldi had chosen a new publisher, Etienne Roger in Amsterdam. There were at least two significant reasons for the switch: superior printing methods and an increased demand for the music of Vivaldi and other Italians in northern Europe. The Sonatas, Op. 5 were actually engraved and published at Roger's own expense. Such a practice was quite rare in Vivaldi's time and testifies to his immense popularity.

Sonata No. 13

The *Sarabanda* (found on page 30) lacks the lasciviously strong accent on the second beat characteristic of the Spanish *sarabande*. Keep the tempo slow, the meter even and play with as much vibrato as possible.

Sonata No. 14

For the *Gavotta* (found on page 32), the left-hand slurs (as in mm. 7-9 and 39-41) may require some extra attention during practice. Isolate each slur and treat it as a trilling exercise. Devote a few minutes each day to these passages until they sound crisp and clear.

Sonata No. 16

In the *Preludio* (found on page 35), exaggerate the dotted rhythms and apply vibrato liberally. Because of the slow tempo, it will be necessary to think ahead and be aware of the melody's direction and shape. At some point, you may want to do a simple phrase analysis of the *Preludio*. Break the piece into small phrases, study how they relate to one another and then group them into longer phrases. The longer the phrases you envision, the better the sense of forward motion you will convey.

Sonata No. 18

The *Air-Minuet* (found on page 38) demonstrates an ambiguity in Vivaldi's choice of titles for movements. The designation "Air" suggests the vocal-like quality of the melody. The piece is also an instrumental dance movement, containing the clear four-bar phrasing and clear cadences typical of a *minuet*. Overall, the piece should sound stately, yet singing.

Il cimento dell'armonia e dell'inventione, Op. 8

The Concertos, Op. 8 were first published in 1725 and dedicated to the Bohemian Count Wenzeslaus von Morzin. The first four concertos are collectively known as "The Four Seasons." A significant feature in each of these concertos is the inclusion of an explanatory sonnet, each line of poetry corresponding to a particular passage in the music.

Concerto No. 2

In the *Allegro non molto* (found on page 40), sustain the chords for as long as possible, letting go with the left hand at the last possible moment. Keep the tempo even without letting it drag. Use lots of vibrato and roll chords with the right hand as little as possible. The corresponding text of the sonnet paints the scene, "In this season of the blazing sun, man and flock swelter while the pines are seared."

Concerto No. 4

For the *Largo* (found on page 42), in order to emulate the violin, the instrument for which this work was originally conceived, the melody needs to sound as smooth and legato as possible. Using lots of vibrato will help to add shape and direction to the melody. The score contains the descriptive text, "To remain quiet and content by the fireside, while outside the rain pours in torrents."

Concertos for Flute, Op. 10

Vivaldi's Concertos for Flute, Op. 10 were first published in 1728 and were very nearly the first published works of their kind. The famous French flautist Louis Boismortier preceded Vivaldi by only one year with the publication of his Six Concertos for Flute, Op. 15 in 1727.

Concerto No. 3

This concerto, "Il Gardellino" ("The Goldfinch"), like "The Four Seasons," is one of the few works of Vivaldi to contain an extramusical reference. It will be interesting to compare the *Largo* of this concerto (found on page 22) to the *Largo* of the Concerto for Flute and Oboe, RV 95 (found on page 68), the movement from which it is drawn.

Concerto No. 4

The *Largo* (found on page 78) contains a ritournello, an orchestral refrain separating statements by the soloist. The chordal passages in mm. 1-2, 6-7, 11-12 and 17-18 represent the ritournello, originally designated to a string orchestra, and should be played in a steady tempo with a strong, full tone. The remaining passages, representing the soloist, can be played with a more subtle and expressive tone. Be sure to make the melody as singing as possible.

Il pastor fido, Op. 13

The authenticity of *Il pastor fido,* Op. 13, a set of six solo sonatas, is rather dubious. After the publication of his Op. 12, Vivaldi, always a shrewd businessman, concluded that he could make a larger profit if he stopped having his works published and instead sold through himself manuscript copies of his works. The Sonatas, Op. 13 were published in Paris in 1737 and believed by many to be clever pastiches of individual movements appropriated from Vivaldi and other popular composers. Two of the possible solo instruments suggested for the Sonatas are French in origin and were virtually unknown in Italy: the *musette* (a French bagpipe) and the *vielle* (a French hurdy-gurdy). Overall, the Sonatas of *Il pastor fido* exhibit a slightly richer harmonic language than what one usually finds in Vivaldi's music.

Sonata No. 6

In the *Largo* (found on page 80), bring out the counterpoint, being especially sensitive to the bass line.

Sonatas for Winds

Sonata for Flute, RV 48

In the *Affetuoso* (found on page 44), keep the melodic line supple and fluid. The *Allegro assai* (found on page 46) contains syncopated passages (such as mm. 43-49). Emphasize the counterpoint by sustaining each note for its full duration. Keep the *Allegro* (found on page 50) at a relatively fast tempo. Special care will have to be taken in areas where both voices contain fast notes, as in mm. 21-33, 44-54 and 66-82. Strive to make both voices sound clear and legato.

Sonata for Flute, RV 49

In the *Preludio* (found on page 54), hang on to notes for as long as possible, especially at cadence points involving suspensions. Play the *Siciliana* (found on page 58) at a slow, even tempo and with a syrupy vibrato. The *Sarabanda* (found on page 56) contains a *petite reprise,* a device borrowed from the French in which the final phrase of the piece is repeated. Be sure to perform this short passage differently each time. Accenting the second beat, typical of the French sarabande, would be appropriate in this *Sarabanda.*

Sonata for Recorder, RV 52

In the *Preludio* (found on page 61), keep the melody clear and singing. In the *Allemanda* (found on page 62), make sure the passages with repeated slurs (as in mm. 4-7) are executed with rhythmic precision. This lively piece should remain dynamically very strong throughout. The *Aria di Giga* (found on page 65) should be fast and lively. The designation "Aria" refers to the singability of the melody.

Concertos for Various Instruments

Concerto for Lute and Two Violins, RV 93

In the *Largo* (found on page 66),the bass voice plays an accompanimental role and should therefore be played rhythmically even. In arpeggiated passages (such as in mm. 9-11 and m. 16), let the notes within chords ring together as much as possible.

Concerto for Flute and Oboe, RV 95

The *Largo* (found on page 68) is true to its nickname ("La Pastorella") and quite pastoral in character, containing a rhythm characteristic of pastoral music (dotted eighth-sixteenth-eighth). Keep the melody very legato and singing.

Concerto for Flute, RV429

In the *Andante* (found on page 70), keep the trills light and quick. The piece should be in a moderate tempo and exhibit a dance-like character.

Concerto for Violin and Organ, RV 541

In the *Grave* (found on page 72), keep the tempo very slow but even. Use lots of vibrato and exploit the full range of dynamic potential in this very expressive piece.

Concerto for Violin and Oboe, RV 543

In the *Allegro alla Francese* (found on page 74), the designation "alla Francese" refers to the piece's *gigue*-like character. Compare this French-style piece to the Italian-style *gigas* on pages 8 and 16. Take the piece at a speedy tempo and accent the downbeat, counting one beat (not three) per measure.

Concerto for Violin and Oboe, RV 548

The *Largo* (found on page 76) is conducive to a wide dynamic range. Areas where the texture is dangerously thin (as in m. 12) can actually be very expressive when handled sensitively. In these passages, keep the tone very warm and rich and experiment with creating some subtle dynamic nuances. Throughout the piece, maintain an awareness of the shape and direction of the melodic line.

About the Arranger

Joseph Harris received his bachelor's and master's degrees in guitar performance at Northern Arizona University as a student of Tom Sheeley. Joseph has done further graduate study in music theory at the University of Iowa. In addition to his work with the classical guitar, his musical pursuits include jazz guitar, music aesthetics and the music of French composer Olivier Messiaen (1908-1992). In his spare time Joseph enjoys camping, canoeing, spelunking and rock climbing.

Explanation of Ornaments

Ornamentation is an indispensible element of music of the Baroque period (approximately 1600-1750). Baroque composers fully expected performers to provide additional notes to those printed in the score. Although the most visible effect of ornamentation is the decoration of the musical surface, ornamentation primarily fulfills two important expressive functions: the creation of dissonance, which defines and strengthens both rhythm and meter, and the suggestion of a particular mood or affect. On an instrument with limited sustaining ability, such as the modern guitar, ornaments sometimes play a third, pragmatic role. With the help of ornamentation, a performer can artificially prolong structurally important notes and fill in spaces in the musical texture.

When performing Baroque music, it is important to remember that ornaments begin on the downbeat (not before it). This practice is supported by the fact that an ornament's expressive function is frequently to act as an accented dissonance; consequently, the ornament needs to occur on the accented part of the beat.

The practice of ornamentation can be a very personal and expressive part of a performer's style. Even so, it is important to obey the composer's wishes and not to ignore any indications for ornaments that appear directly in the score. In order not to greatly obscure the notation of the music, Baroque composers used special symbols to indicate different types of ornaments. Below are brief explanations of the ornaments used by Vivaldi and suggestions for their execution.

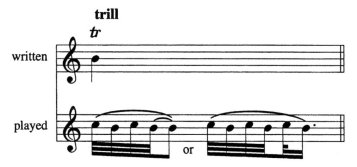

The trill is an alternation between a note and its upper neighbor. The trill should begin simultaneously on the upper note and the downbeat. The number of notes in a trill may vary depending on the tempo of the piece and the duration of the affected note. A wavy line following an indication for a trill (*tr*⌇⌇) indicates an extension.

The appoggiatura contains a single grace note slurred to the main note. The duration of each note should be half the notated value of the main note. Despite its notation, the appoggiatura begins on the downbeat, not before it.

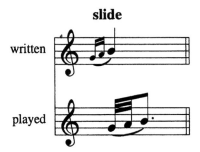

The slide, which is sometimes refered to as *Schleifer* in German and *coulé* in French, is an appoggiatura consisting of two grace notes. Like the appoggiatura, the slide begins on the downbeat.

Adagio
from Sonata for Violin , Op. 2, No. 3

Arranged for guitar by
Joseph Harris

Antonio Vivaldi
(1678-1741)

Giga
from Sonata for Violin, Op. 2, No. 3

Arranged for guitar by
Joseph Harris

Antonio Vivaldi
(1678-1741)

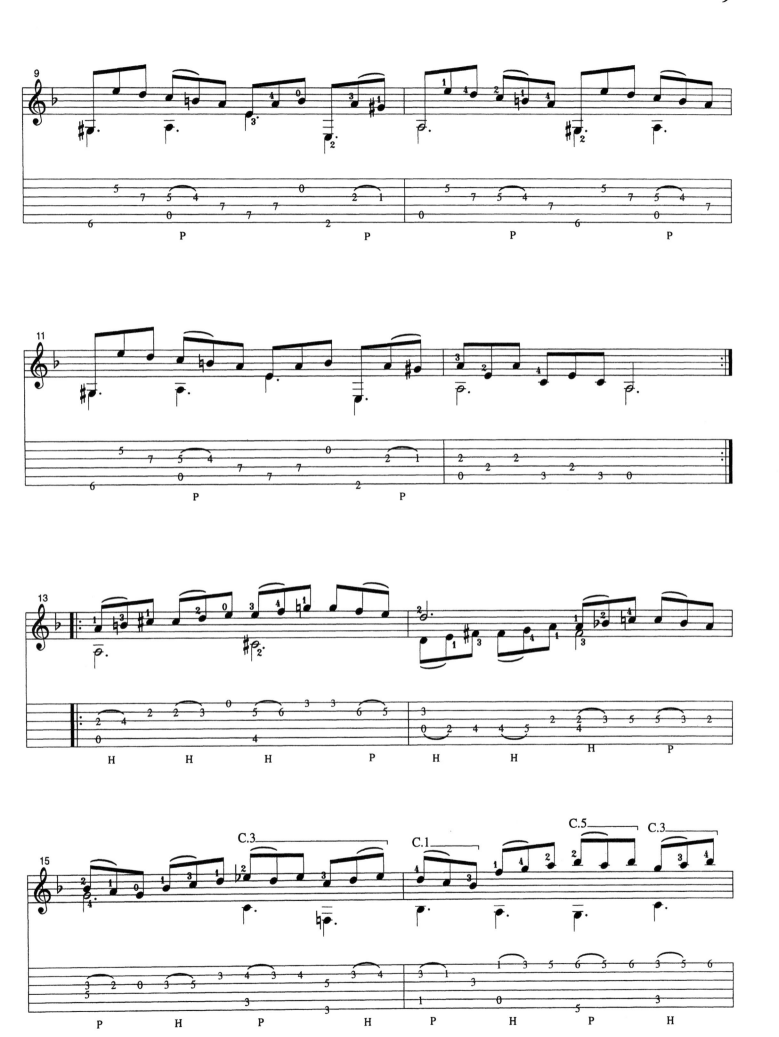

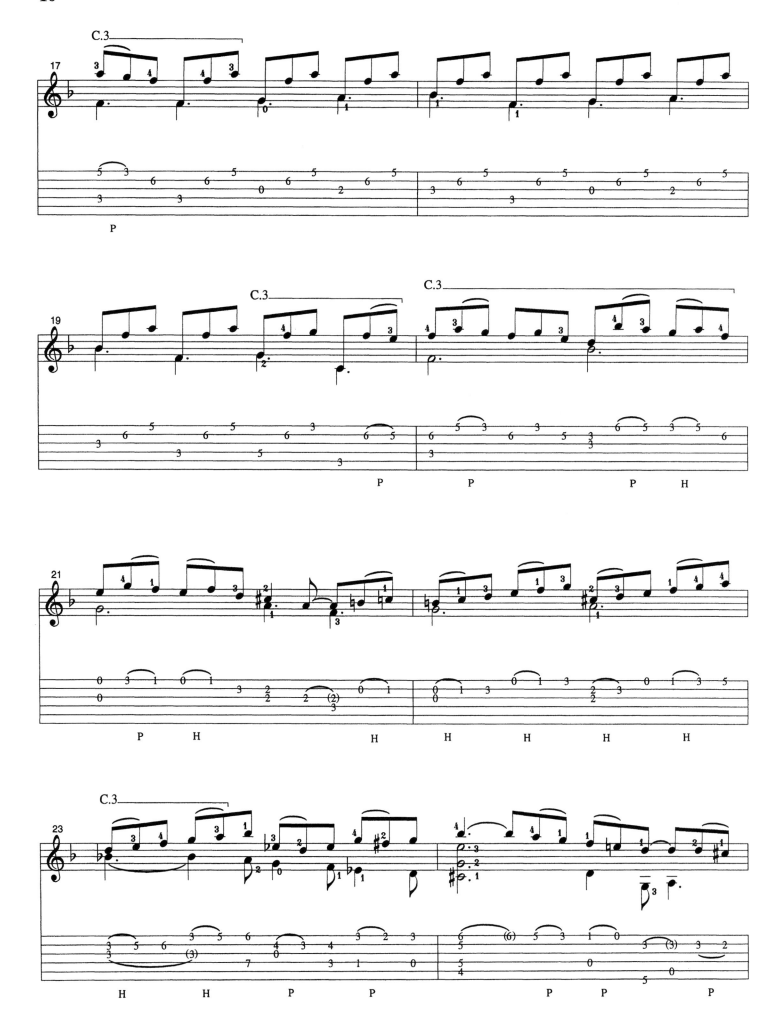

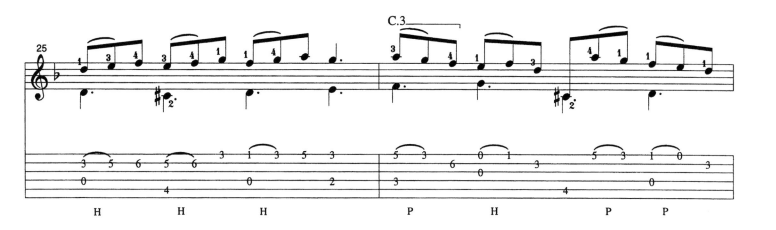

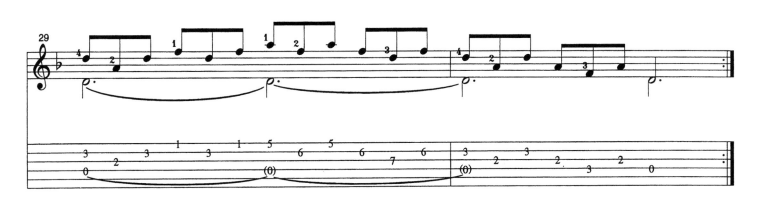

Preludio
from Sonata for Violin, Op. 2, No. 6

Arranged for guitar by
Joseph Harris

Antonio Vivaldi
(1678-1741)

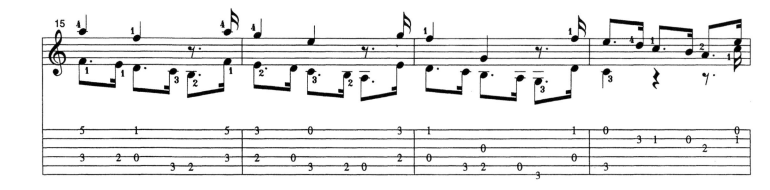

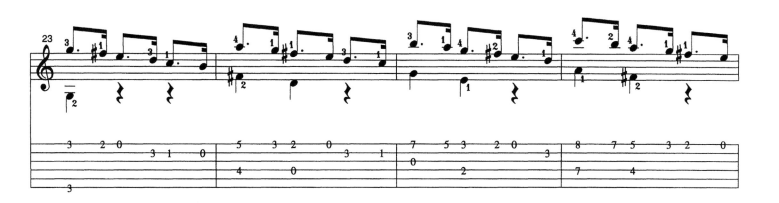

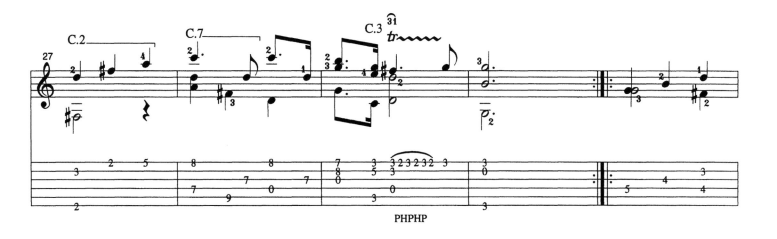

PHP

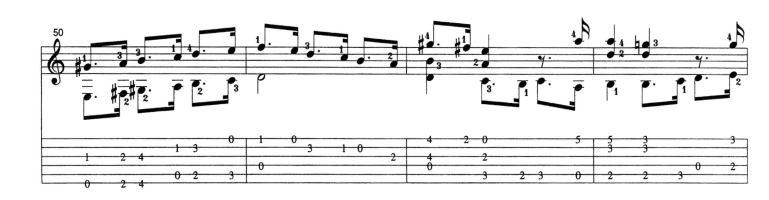

Giga
from Sonata for Violin, Op. 2, No. 6

Arranged for guitar by
Joseph Harris

Antonio Vivaldi
(1678-1741)

Corrente
from Sonata for Violin, Op. 2, No. 7

Arranged for guitar by
Joseph Harris

Antonio Vivaldi
(1678-1741)

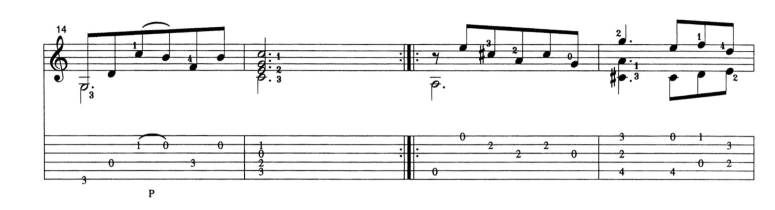

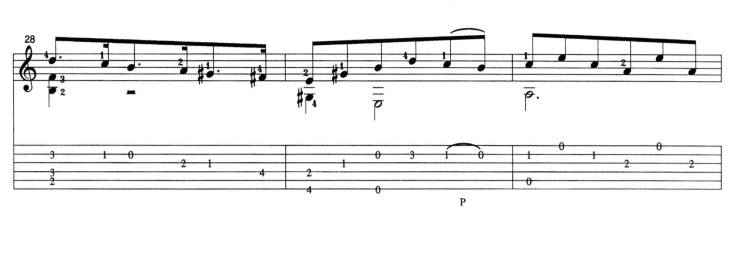

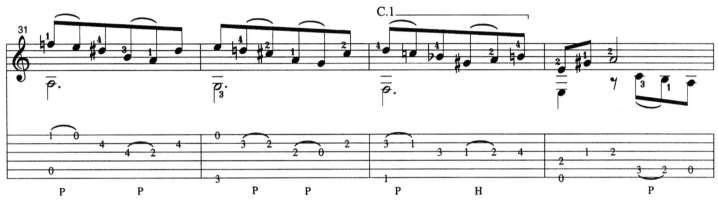

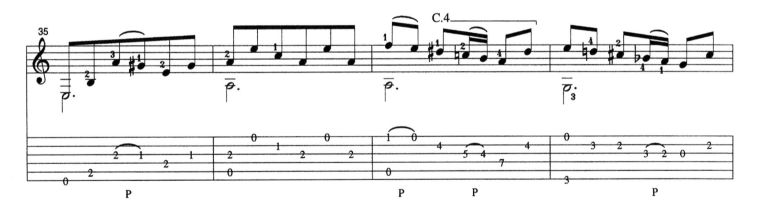

Largo
from Concerto for Flute, Op. 10, No. 3 ("Il Gardellino")

Arranged for guitar by
Joseph Harris

Antonio Vivaldi
(1678-1741)

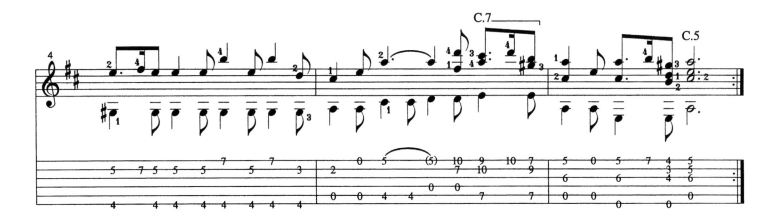

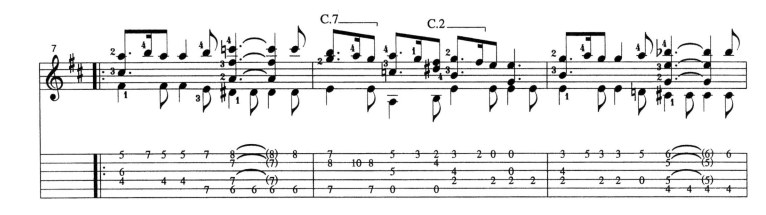

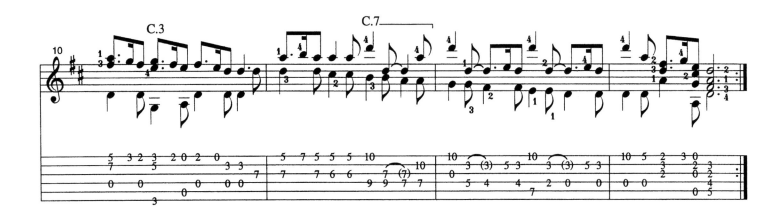

Preludio
from Sonata for Violin, Op. 2, No. 9

Arranged for guitar by
Joseph Harris

Antonio Vivaldi
(1678-1741)

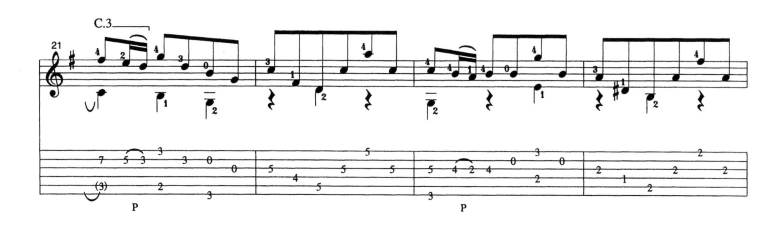

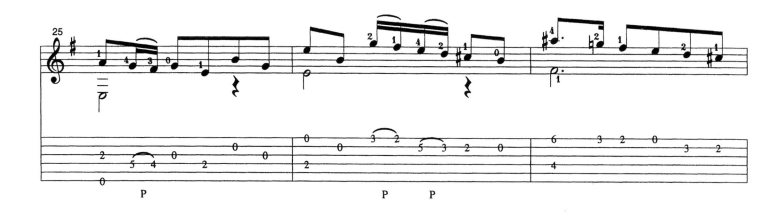

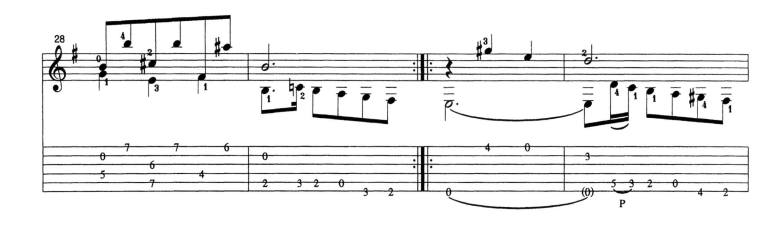

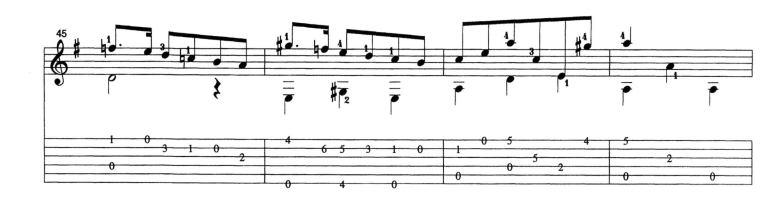

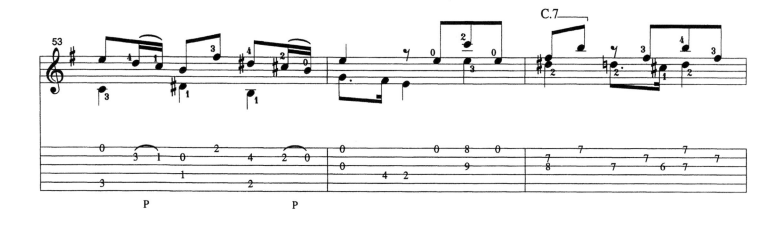

Gavotta
from Sonata for Violin, Op. 2, No. 11

Arranged for guitar by
Joseph Harris

Antonio Vivaldi
(1678-1741)

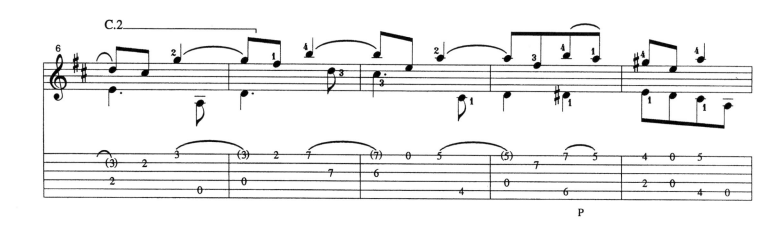

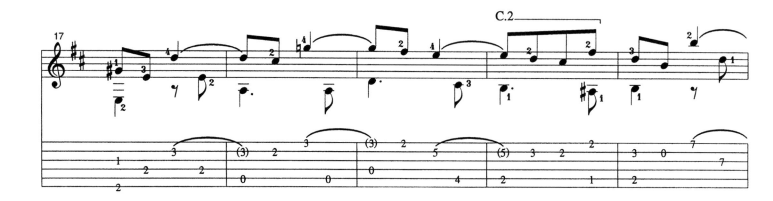

Sarabanda
from Sonata for Violin, Op. 5, No. 13

Arranged for guitar by
Joseph Harris

Antonio Vivaldi
(1678-1741)

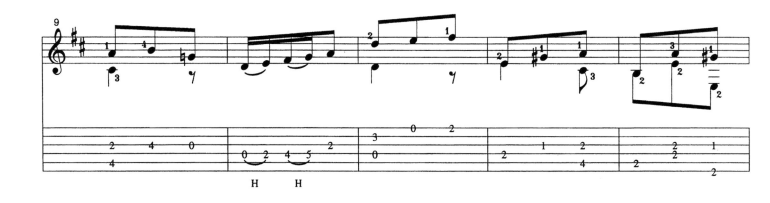

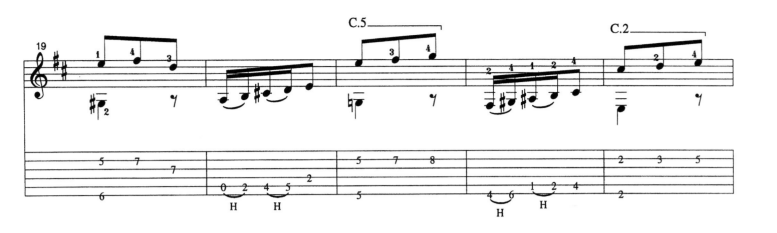

Gavotta
from Sonata for Violin, Op. 5, No. 14

Arranged for guitar by
Joseph Harris

Antonio Vivaldi
(1678-1741)

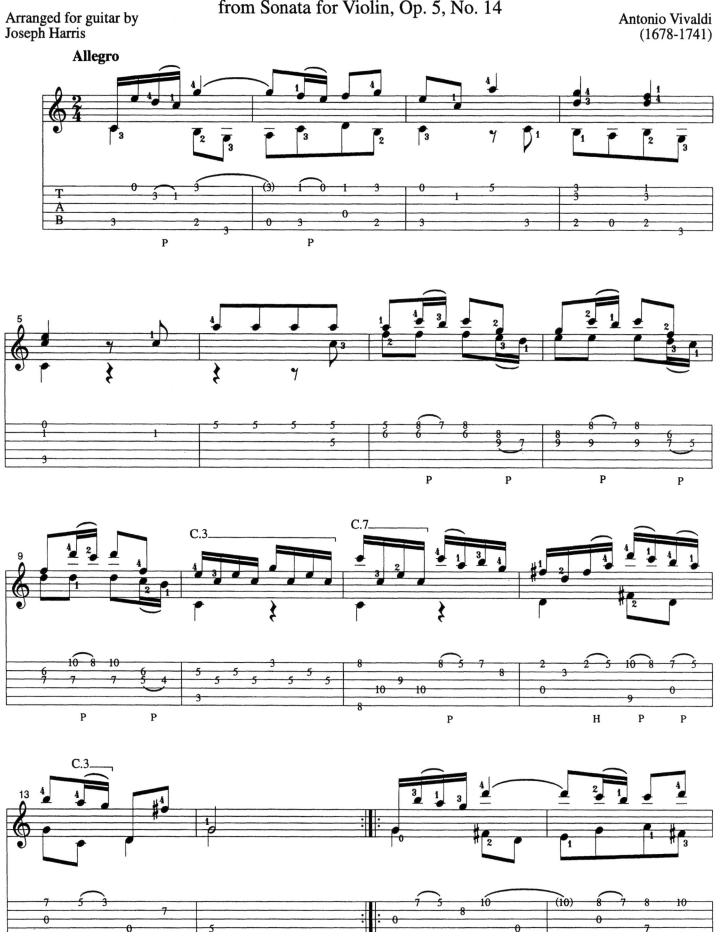

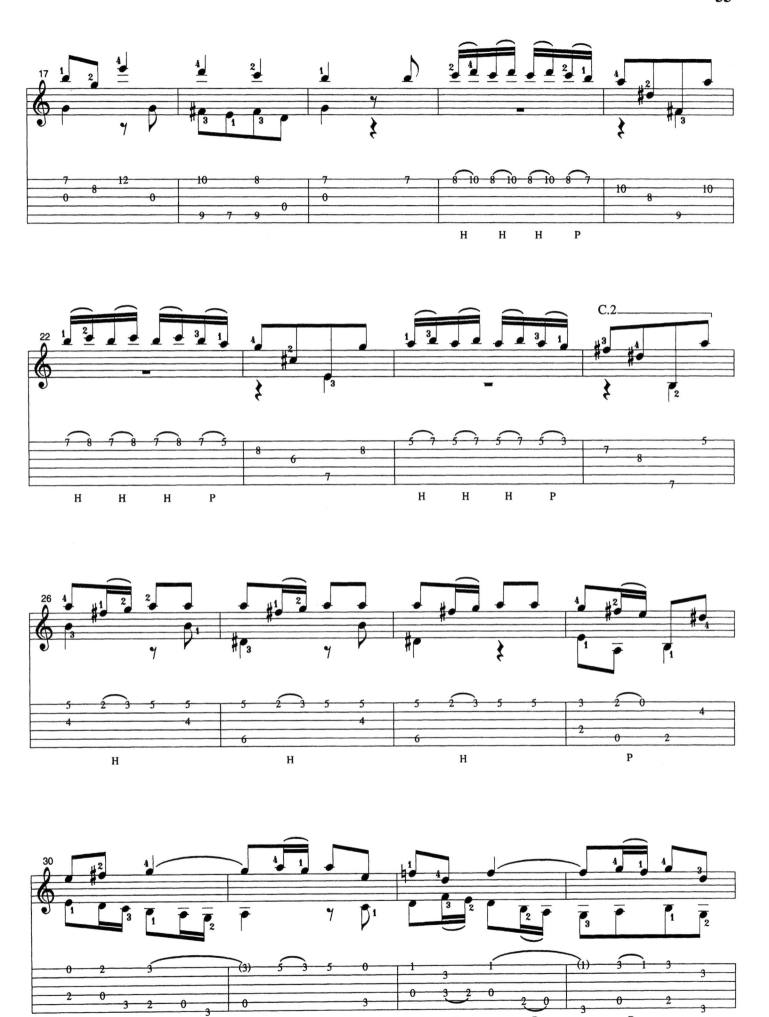

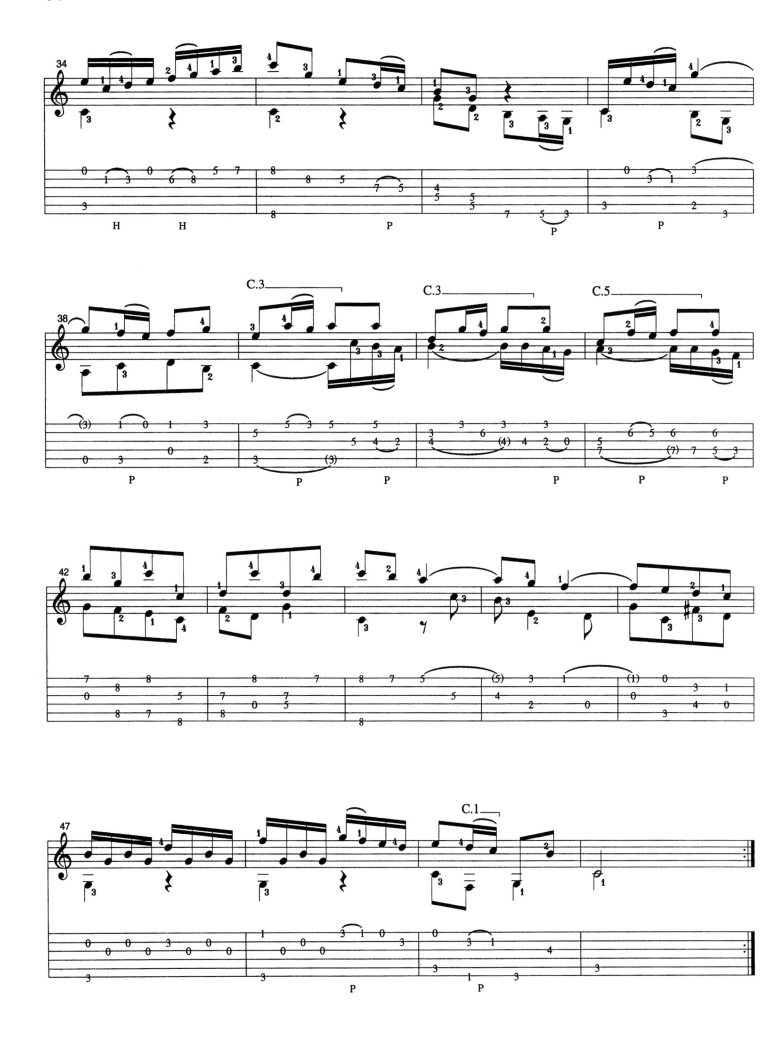

Preludio
from Sonata for Violin, Op. 5, No. 16

Arranged for guitar by
Joseph Harris

Antonio Vivaldi
(1678-1741)

Air-Menuet
from Sonata for Two Violins, Op. 5, No. 18

Arranged for guitar by
Joseph Harris

Antonio Vivaldi
(1678-1741)

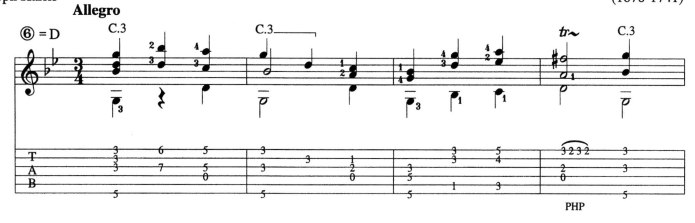

PHP

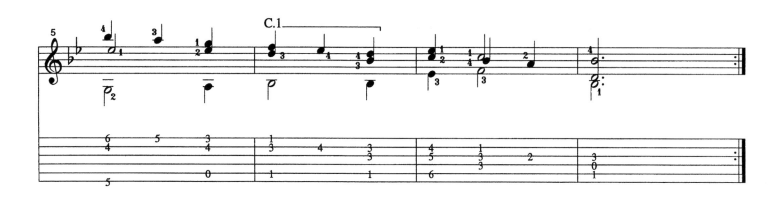

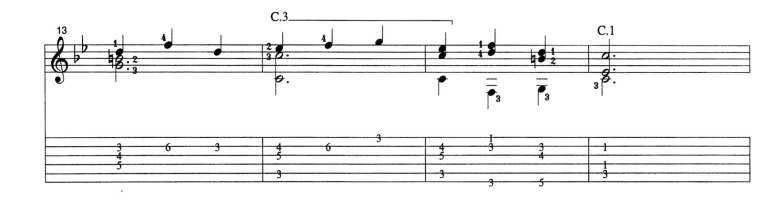

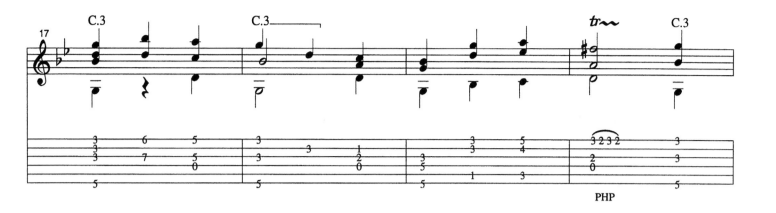

Allegro non molto
from *The Four Seasons,* Op. 8, No. 2 ("Summer")

Arranged for guitar by
Joseph Harris

Antonio Vivaldi
(1678-1741)

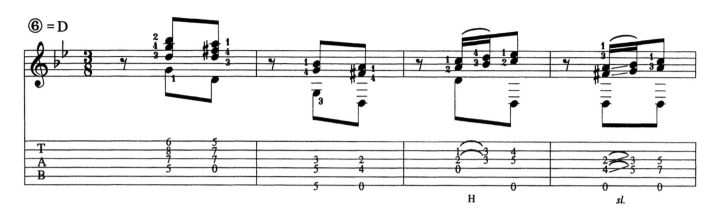

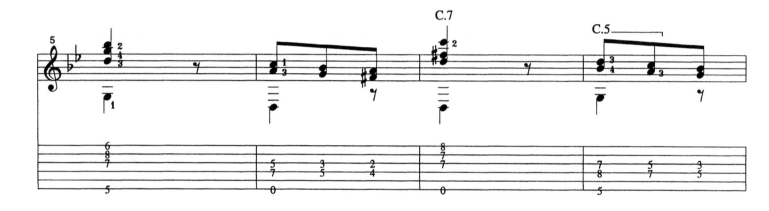

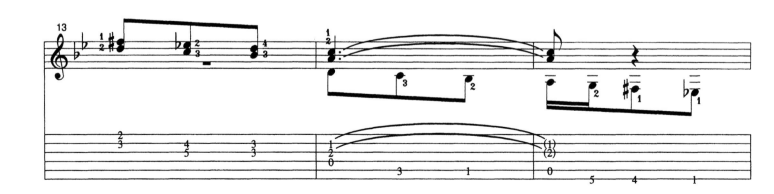

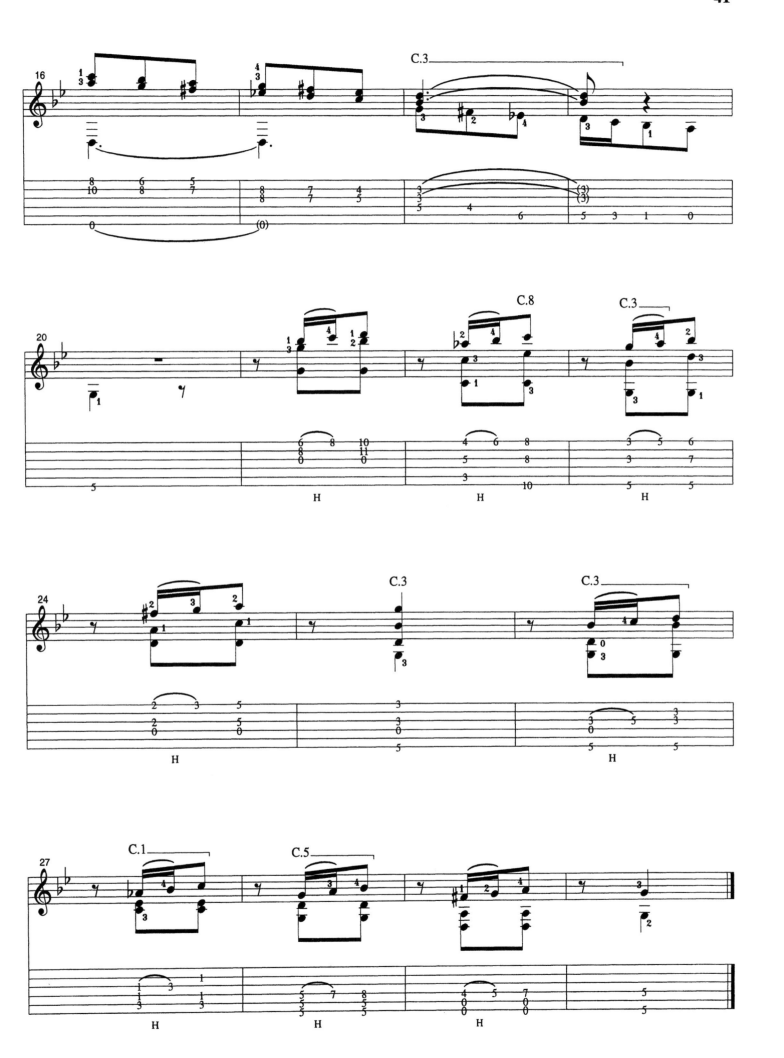

Largo
from *The Four Seasons*, Op. 8, No. 4 ("Winter")

Arranged for guitar
by Joe Harris

Antonio Vivaldi
(1685-1741)

Affettuoso
from Sonata for Flute, RV 48

Arranged for guitar by
Joseph Harris

Antonio Vivaldi
(1678-1741)

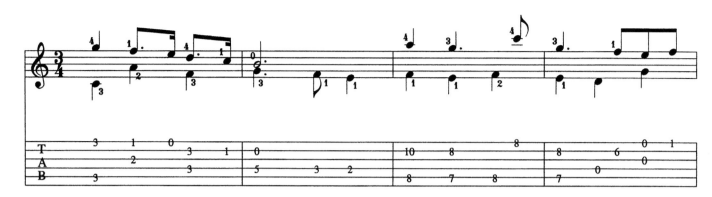

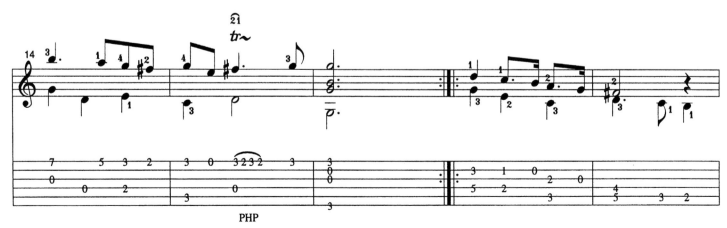

Allegro assai
from Sonata for Flute, RV 48

Arranged for guitar by
Joseph Harris

Antonio Vivaldi
(1678-1741)

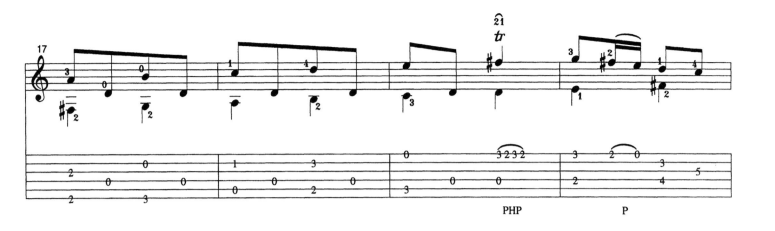

Allegro
from Sonata for Flute, RV 48

Arranged for guitar
by Joe Harris

Antonio Vivaldi
(1675-1741)

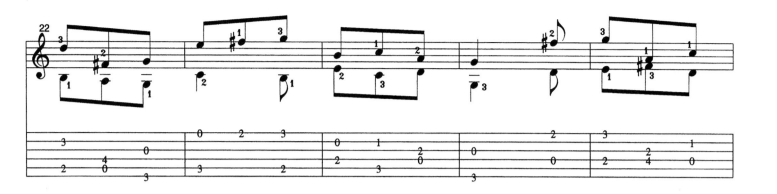

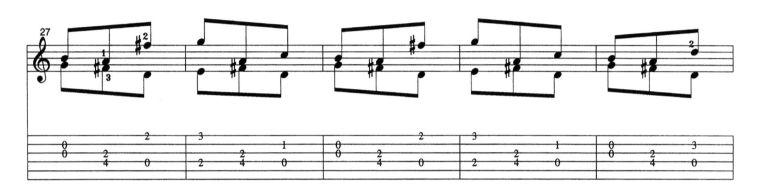

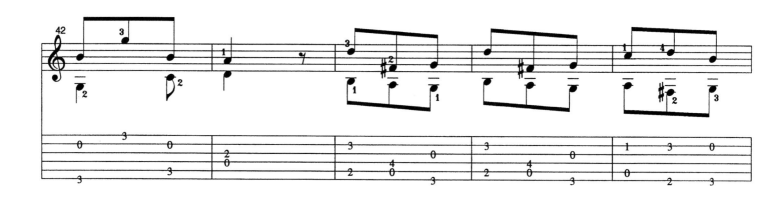

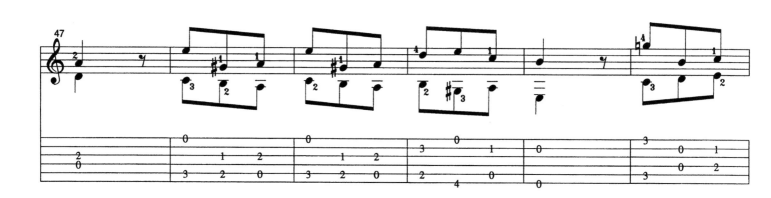

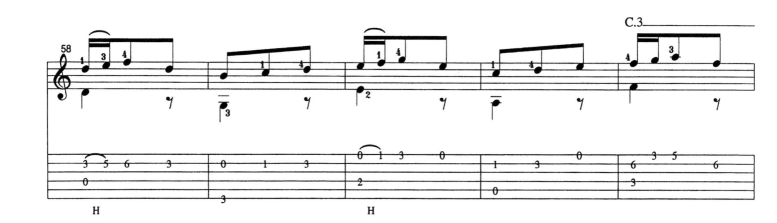

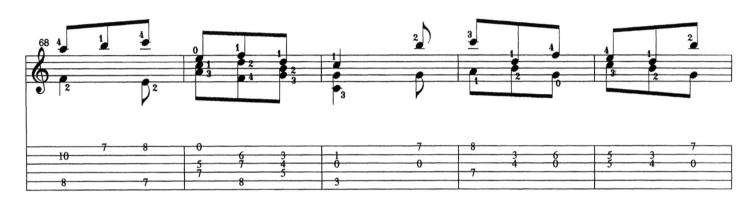

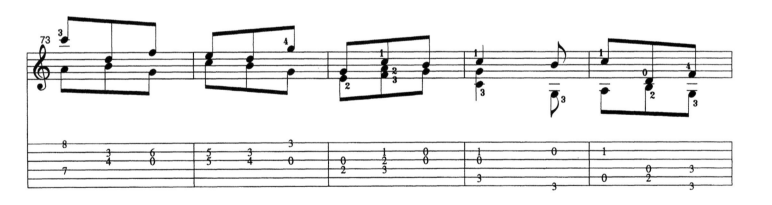

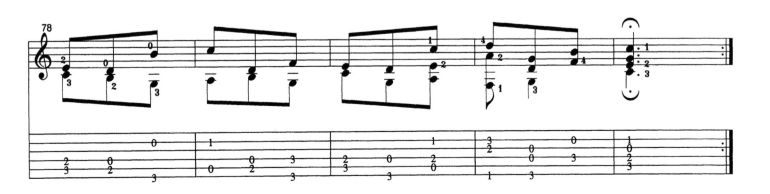

Preludio
from Sonata for Flute, RV 49

Arranged for guitar by
Joseph Harris

Antonio Vivaldi
(1678-1741)

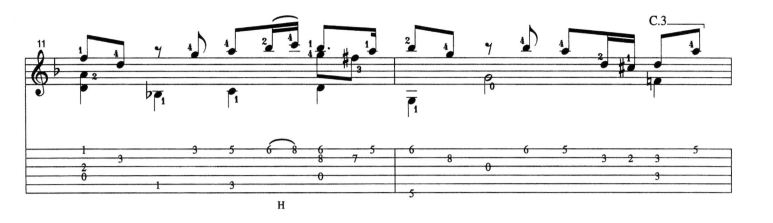

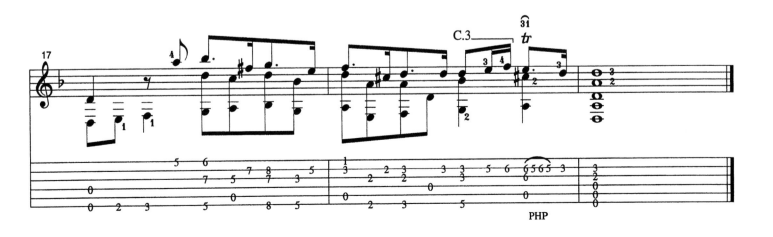

Sarabanda
from Sonata for Flute, RV 49

Arranged for guitar by
Joseph Harris

Antonio Vivaldi
(1678-1741)

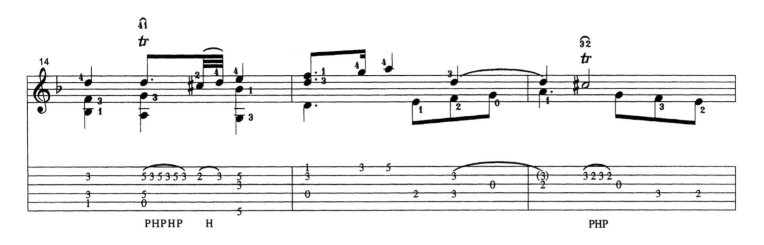

PHPHP   H   PHP

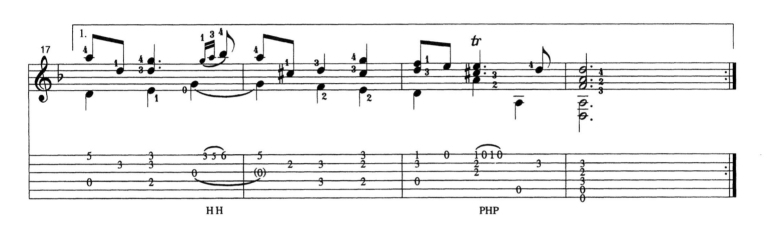

H H   PHP

H H   PHP

H H   PHP

Siciliana
from Sonata for Flute, RV 49

Arranged for guitar by
Joseph Harris

Antonio Vivaldi
(1678-1741)

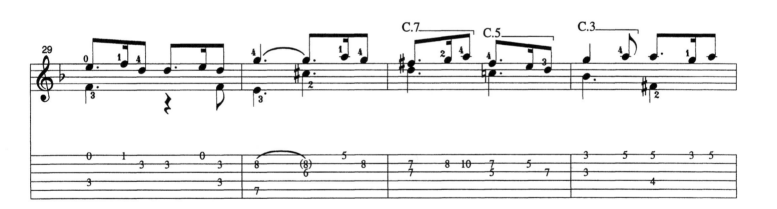

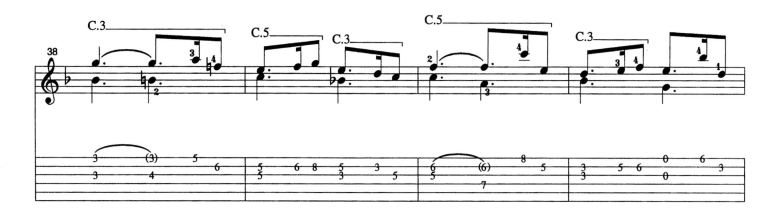

Preludio
from Sonata for Recorder, RV 52

Arranged for guitar by
Joseph Harris

Antonio Vivaldi
(1678-1741)

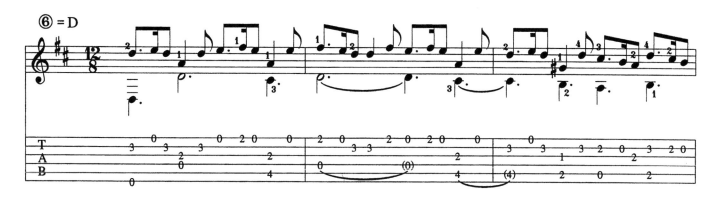

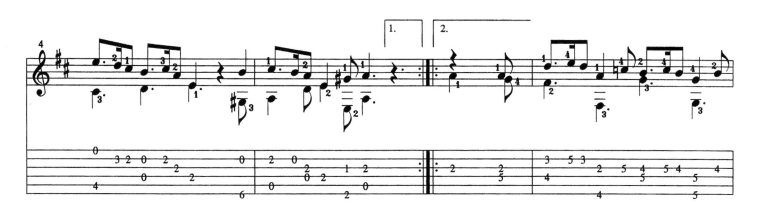

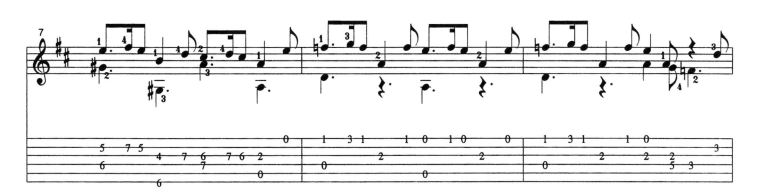

Allemanda
from Sonata for Recorder, RV 52

Arranged for guitar by
Joseph Harris

Antonio Vivaldi
(1678-1741)

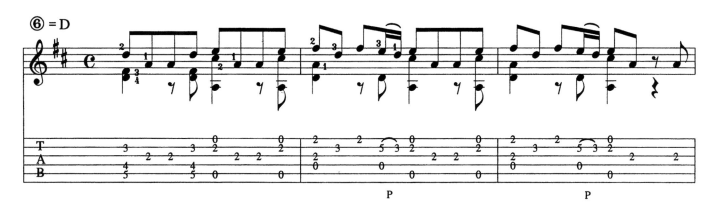

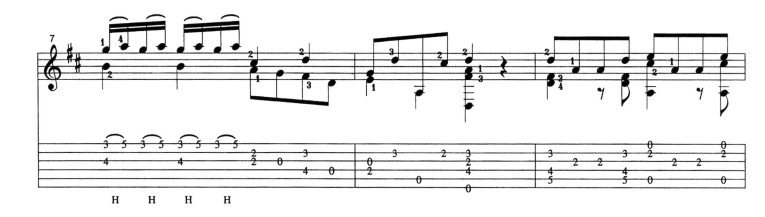

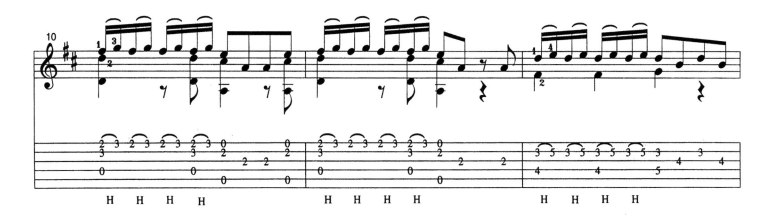

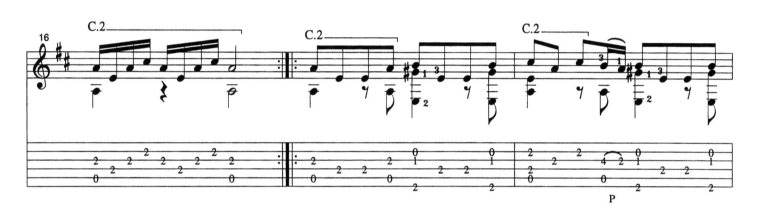

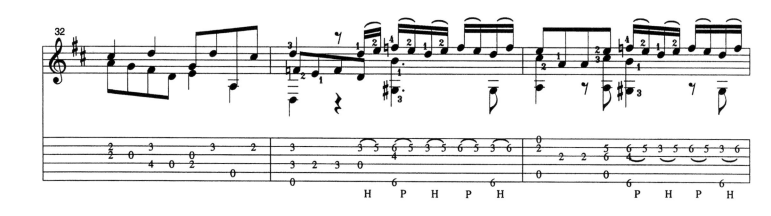

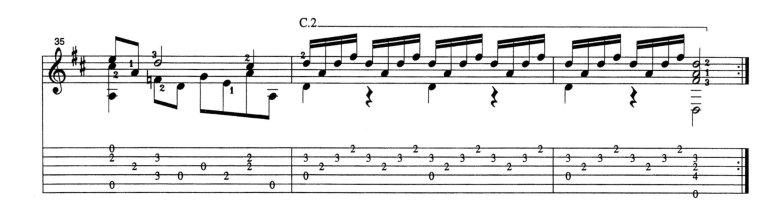

Aria di Giga
from Sonata for Recorder, RV 52

Arranged for guitar by
Joseph Harris

Antonio Vivaldi
(1678-1741)

Largo
from Concerto for Lute and Two Violins, RV 93

Arranged for guitar
by Joe Harris

Antonio Vivaldi
(1675-1741)

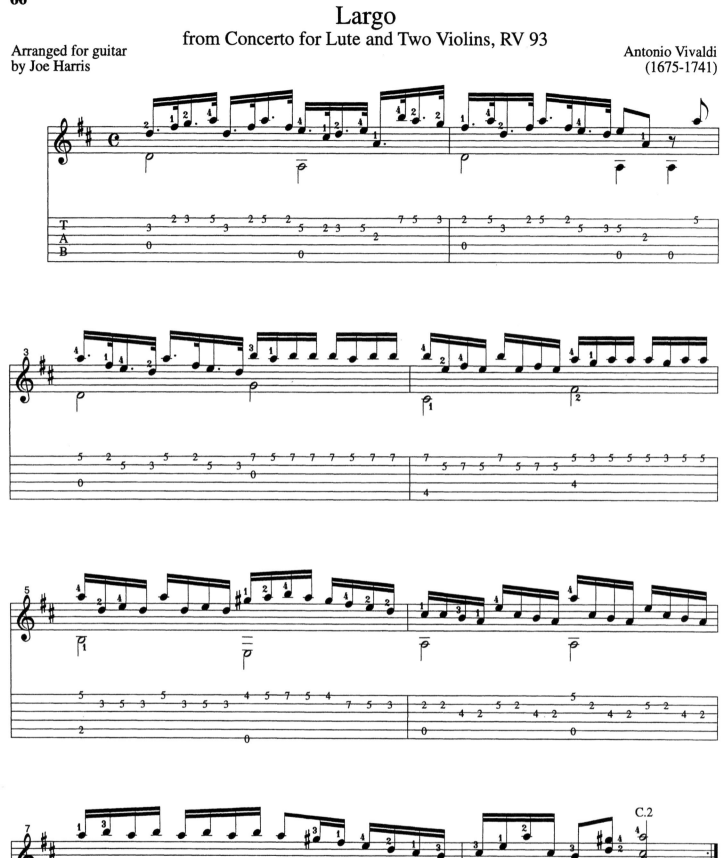

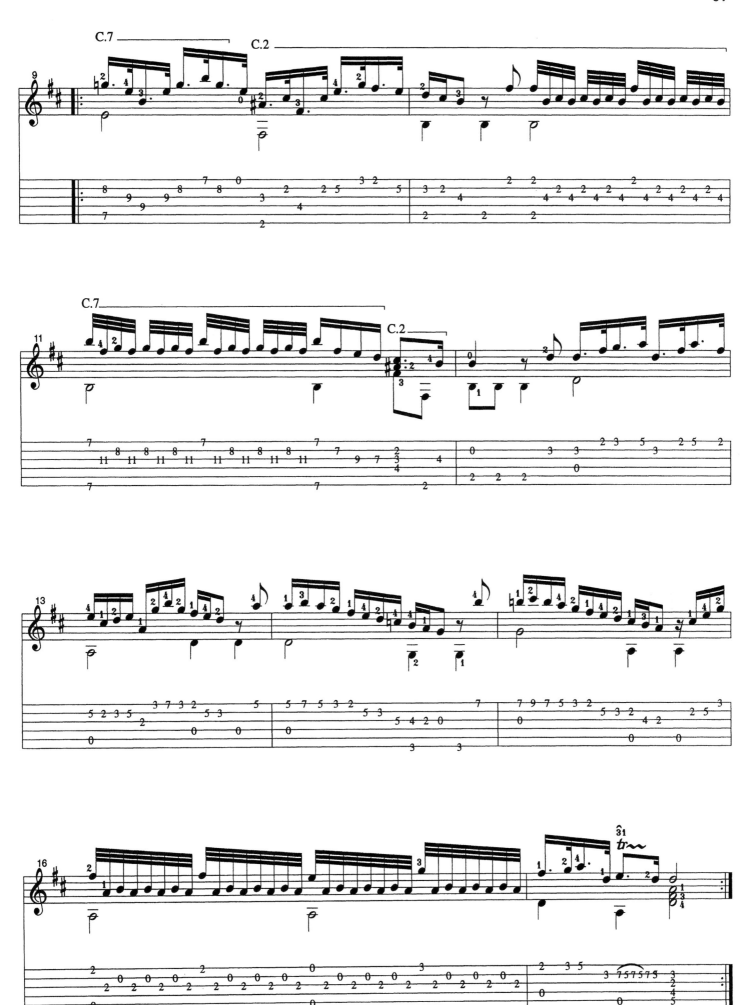

PHPHP

Largo
from Concerto for Flute and Oboe, RV 95 ("La Pastorella")

Arranged for guitar by
Joseph Harris

Antonio Vivaldi
(1678-1741)

Andante
from Concerto for Flute, RV 429

Arranged for guitar by
Joseph Harris

Antonio Vivaldi
(1678-1741)

Grave
from Concerto for Violin and Organ, RV 541

Arranged for guitar by
Joseph Harris

Antonio Vivaldi
(1678-1741)

Allegro alla Francese
from Concerto for Violin and Oboe, RV 543

Arranged for guitar by
Joseph Harris

Antonio Vivaldi
(1678-1741)

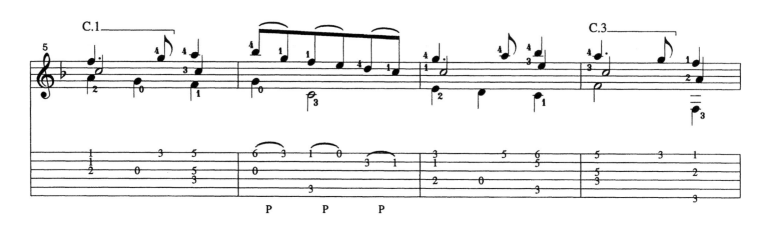

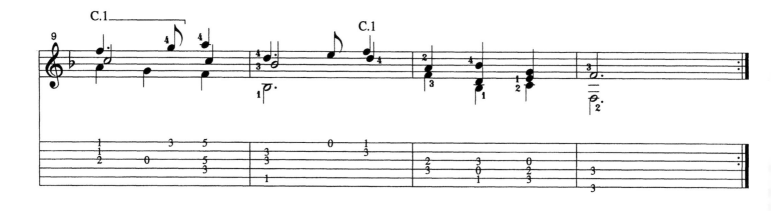

Largo
from Concerto for Oboe and Violin, RV 548

Arranged for guitar by
Joseph Harris

Antonio Vivaldi
(1678-1741)

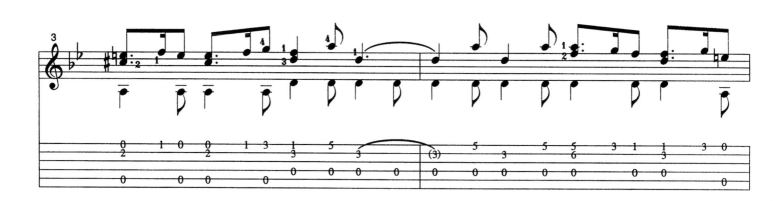

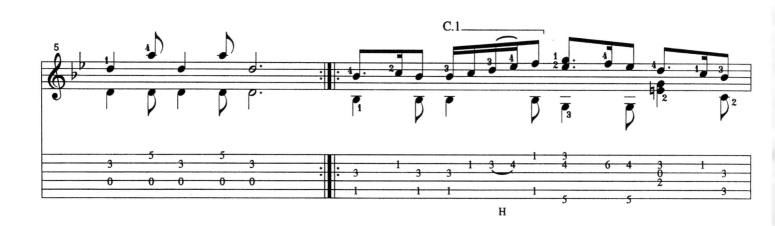

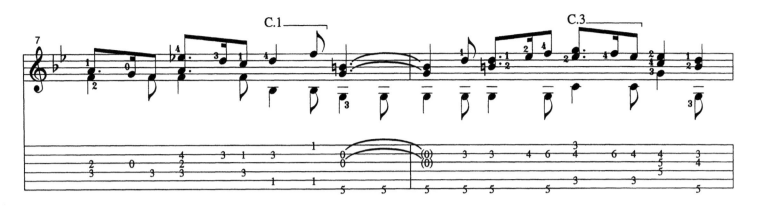

Largo
from Concerto for Flute, Op. 10, No. 4

Arranged for guitar by
Joseph Harris

Antonio Vivaldi
(1678-1741)

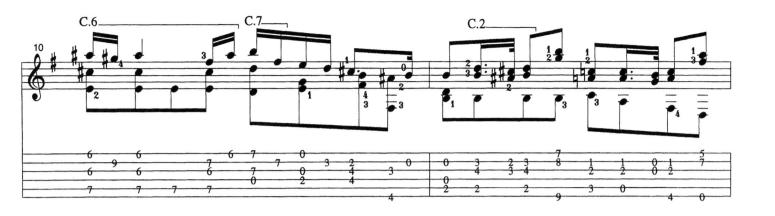

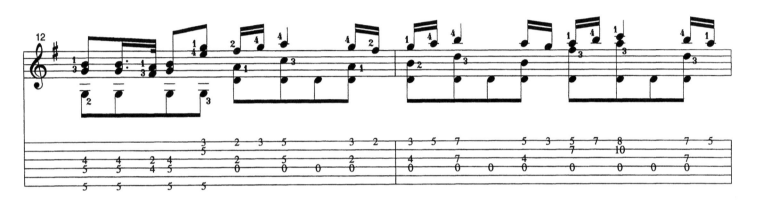

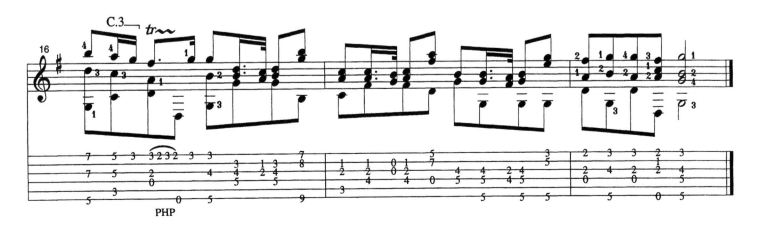

Largo
from Sonata for Musette, Vielle, Flute, Oboe or Violin, Op. 13, No. 6

Arranged for guitar by
Joseph Harris

Antonio Vivaldi
(1678-1741)